The Mirror of Love

THE MIRROR OF LOVE

Readings with Margery Kempe

Introduced and edited by
Gillian Hawker

MOREHOUSE PUBLISHING
Harrisburg, PA

Introduction and arrangement
© 1988 Gillian Hawker

First published in Great Britain by
Darton, Longman and Todd Ltd.

First published in America by: **Morehouse Publishing**

Editorial Office:
871 Ethan Allen Highway
Ridgefield, CT 06877

Corporate Office:
P.O. Box 1321
Harrisburg, PA 17105

Library of Congress Cataloging-in-Publication Data
Kempe, Margery, b. ca. 1373.
    The mirror of love: daily readings with Margery Kempe /
introduced and edited by Gillian Hawker.
        p.   cm.
    Includes bibliographical references and index.
    ISBN 0-8192-1575-9 (pbk.)
    1. Meditations—Early works to 1800.   2. Kempe,
Margery, b. ca. 1373.   I. Title
BX2181.K45   1991   91-18023
242'.2—dc20   CIP

Printed in the United States of America
by
BSC LITHO
Harrisburg, PA 17105

Contents

Introduction

Margery Kempe was a visionary. She had a mental image of God with whom she walked and talked on her pilgrimage. *The Book*, as Margery called it, is her spiritual journal.

Margery is not a teacher. She is a fourteenth-century housewife and a lay member of the Church who had deep spiritual experiences. Through her book we catch a glimpse of the teaching and influences of her time.

Born *c.* 1373 in the town of Bishop's Lynn (now King's Lynn) Margery was the daughter of a prosperous merchant, John Brunham. He was at various times mayor and local member of parliament. Despite her father's position Margery could neither read nor write.

Although technically illiterate, Margery was certainly not uneducated. She possessed a phenomenal memory, absorbing the contents of books, sermons and conversations like blotting paper, and was able to recall them in detail more than twenty years later. She persuaded clerics to read to her from the Bible and the spiritual writers of her day among whom she mentions Richard Rolle, Walter Hilton and St Bridget, with whom she had a particular affinity.

The Book was dictated to a clerk who added a page of his own in explanation (the proem). Throughout her book Margery refers to herself as 'that creature'. I have taken the liberty of using the personal pronoun for ease of devotional reading.

Margery starts her book with her marriage at

about the age of twenty to John Kempe. He was a burgess of the town, although not such an exalted figure as her father. Soon after, 'as nature would', she gives birth to her first child. We are not told the sex of the baby; to Margery the significance of the event was the severe post-natal depression which followed. She is cured when Jesus appears to her in a vision, gently rebuking her with the words, 'Daughter, why hast thou forsaken me, when I forsook thee never?'.

From that moment Margery desires nothing so much as to follow Jesus, but being human, she finds that it is not a simple ambition. She is disarmingly honest about her backslidings and records instances which illustrate her pride, vanity and sexual temptations.

Her second 'experience with God' comes one night when she is lying beside her husband. She hears music so sweet that she thinks she is in paradise. Leaping out of bed she exclaims, 'Alas, that ever I did sin! It is full merry in heaven.' Ever afterwards the sound of music was likely to provoke tears of love and devotion.

It is after this second visitation that Margery is convinced she should lead a chaste life, but on this point at least her husband remains adamant and somewhat unwillingly she continues to bear him children until there are fourteen in all. Despite the disparaging remarks Margery makes about her husband's lack of means and position, they must have been able to keep a household of servants, for her prayer life would have left her little time for anything else!

Margery claimed that she went to church at

two or three o'clock every morning and remained there until after noon, sometimes making her confession three times a day. The days spent in prayer and contemplation bring further visions and Margery describes how 'in her soul' she becomes a participant in the events of our Lord's life.

Tears were the hallmark of Margery's prayer. She wept for the sorrow that her sins caused our Lord and for the pain he suffered from the wrong-doing of others. She wept for joy at the glimpses of heaven she was given. Most of all she wept during the Mass, for the pain our Lord suffered on the cross. Margery did not weep quietly; her noisy sobbing disturbed the other worshippers and upset the clergy, frequently causing her to be ejected from the church – much to her dismay, for she loved to hear a good sermon. Margery's tears may have embarrassed the clergy and her friends, but her obvious piety gained admiration from the common people who regarded her as a holy woman and asked for her prayers.

Margery's long-suffering husband accompanied her around the country, visiting shrines and abbeys. Eventually she persuaded him to sign a mutual vow of chastity in front of the Bishop of Lincoln, Philip Repington. This released her to fulfil a long-held ambition to visit the Holy Land. Her husband consented on condition that she paid his debts before she left. The death of her father may have given her the money to do this and to pay for her journey.

Before she left, Margery and her husband visited the Archbishop of Canterbury, Thomas

Arundel, at Lambeth. Margery told the Archbishop about her visions and her way of life. He readily agreed to give her a letter of authority to choose her own confessor and receive communion every Sunday – an unusual privilege for a lay person.

Margery visited Dame Julian of Norwich, with whom many will be familiar through her *Revelations of Divine Love* and the extracts from it in *Enfolded in Love* in this series. To have a written account from someone who actually talked with Julian makes fascinating reading for her devotees. Extracts from their conversation are included in this book. Also included are words of advice from William Southfield, a Carmelite friar from Norwich, whom Margery visited.

Margery probably left for the Holy Land in the autumn of 1414 – her book is written as she recalled events, rather than in chronological order. She embarked from Yarmouth, one of the towns licensed for the departure of pilgrims. She tells very little about her journey, only recording the trials and tribulations she encountered with her travelling companions. Margery's pilgrimage was undertaken in a spirit of piety at the command of the Lord and she does not hesitate to say so, to the annoyance of those who, like Chaucer's pilgrims in the *Canterbury Tales*, regarded their licence as permission for a holiday.

Margery approached the city of Jerusalem riding on an ass. She was so overwhelmed by her first glimpse of the city that she would have fallen off had it not been for the help of two German pilgrims. Throughout her travels Margery is

10

treated with more kindness and courtesy by for-
eigners than by her compatriots.

The book is not a travelogue. Margery does not
describe the holy places; for her, their importance
lay in the impact they made upon her. At the
Mount of Calvary, 'in her soul', as she is always
careful to say, she saw the crucifixion enacted
before her eyes; she fell to the ground with
outstretched arms, writhing in an agony of grief
and, as she says, 'crying with a loud voice which
sapped all (her) strength'. For the next ten years,
any mention of the Passion, or anything even
remotely connected with it, triggered off the same
violent response.

Margery spent three weeks in the Holy Land,
visiting and weeping at all the shrines. On her
return journey she stopped at Assisi and then
Rome where she spent several months. In Rome
Margery was able to see the room where St
Bridget died, and she spoke to the woman who
had tended her in her last days.

It was in Rome that Margery started wearing
the white clothes which marked her out for the
rest of her life. The Lord had urged her to adopt
this mode of dress long before, but she had
demurred. Now, in gratitude for a safe journey,
she accepted the white clothing that identified her
as chosen by God.

Margery's second pilgrimage was to Santiago
de Compostela. Her implicit faith that the Lord
would provide means for her to go is rewarded,
even to the extent that she is able to repay money
that she borrowed in Rome. Margery tells us little
about her trip except that she stayed two weeks

11

and that the weather was fair both ways – a matter of importance to a bad sailor!

Returning to Bristol, Margery contrived to visit Hayles Abbey in Gloucestershire where a relic of the holy blood was kept. From there she went to Leicester, where she was arrested as a Lollard. Leicester had recently been the setting for Lollard trials and any behaviour outside the norm was likely to arouse suspicion.

She was acquitted and allowed to proceed to York. Here she was arrested again and dragged before the Archbishop. He questioned her on the articles of faith and was forced to be satisfied with her orthodox answers, despite which he urged her to leave the area. Attempting to do so, she was re-arrested, and we can almost hear the Archbishop groan, 'Not you again, woman!'. At her suggestion, the Archbishop gives Margery a letter of passage, bearing his seal, and as an extra precaution provides her with an escort to see her safely across the Humber.

For the next eight years Margery suffered recurrent bouts of illness. At one point she was anointed, but God assured her that she would not die yet. As she recovered, her crying and weeping increased, and the priests took to giving her her communion in the prior's chapel out of earshot of other people. This continued until her violent fits of crying stopped as suddenly as they had started. Margery found the derision occasioned by her quieter demeanour almost harder to bear than the jeering to which she had become accustomed. Now people were quite convinced that she could have controlled her outbursts all along. She turned to the Lord for comfort and he gently reminded her that only he knew what was in her heart.

Margery's prayer life was interrupted when her ageing husband sustained severe head injuries after falling down the stairs. For some time they had been living apart, to avoid gossip claiming that their vow of chastity was a sham. Now, somewhat unwillingly, she took her husband home to look after him.

Hurt by malicious tongues blaming her for the accident, Margery was afraid of further recriminations if her husband should die. Torn between her duty, and her desire to spend all her time in prayer, Margery laid her problem before the Lord. The answer may not have been to her liking, but she followed it faithfully. The Lord told her that she could serve him best by caring for her husband.

Margery must have needed all the grace for which she prayed. She tells us that she cared for her husband for years and that he became increasingly senile. We can feel for her in her grumbling about the cost of extra heating and the quantity of washing when he became doubly incontinent. Wearily she lamented that contemplation was almost impossible. Margery found that it helped to make life tolerable if, while tending her husband, she recalled how different he had been in the early days of her marriage. The present trials she came to regard as punishment for her sins, and she strove to care for his body as if it had been Christ's.

The second part of her book is the record of her last pilgrimage. Her son, the only one of the children whom she mentions, returned home with his Dutch wife. Margery's joy at his return was shortlived, as he died soon after his arrival. Not long afterwards her husband also died. Margery was free and with a daughter-in-law who wanted to return to her family in the Low Countries. Now in her sixties, Margery offered to accompany her daughter-in-law to Ipswich, but once there, she was quite convinced that the Lord told her to go further.

Margery spent five or six weeks in Danzig, then she could not resist the opportunity when a man offered to escort her to Wilsnak to see the miraculous hosts. Travelling from Wilsnak to Aachen her escort deserted her and it was only by tagging on to various parties in succession that Margery managed to reach Calais for the return journey.

The Book ends as abruptly as it started. We can only surmise that perhaps Margery spent her remaining years quietly in Lynn. In 1438, an entry in the record book shows that a 'Margery Kempe' was admitted to the Guild of the Trinity of which her father and her husband had both been members – a belated accolade of respectability.

GILLIAN HAWKER
Polperro
Cornwall

1

Trust

The Lord Jesus Christ appeared to me in a vision when I was in distress; he sat on my bedside wearing a cloak of purple silk. He looked at me with so much love that I felt his strength flow into my spirit and he said, 'Why have you forsaken me, when I have never abandoned you?'

Blessed be Jesus who is always near in times of stress. Even when we cannot feel his presence he is close.

Jesus said within my heart, 'I will never leave you either in happiness or distress. I will always be there to help you and watch over you. Nothing in heaven or earth can part you from me.'

'When you are quiet and still I can speak to your heart.'

2

Love

Lord, I am here because I love you; help me and show me what to do.

In my heart I heard Jesus say, 'Love me as I love you. I have chosen you and keep continual watch over you. You cannot solve all your problems without my help.'

'I am within you and you are within me; if people listen to you they will hear my voice. When people are kind to you they are kind to me but if they are unkind to you, then they are unkind to me.'

3

Grace

Jesus said to me, 'My grace in you is like the sun. Sometimes the sun shines brightly so that everyone can see it, at other times it is hidden behind a cloud; although you cannot see it, the brightness is still there. In the same way my grace is always with you.'

'My grace is always with you. Anyone who does the will of God, is my brother and sister and mother (Mark 3:35). When you try to please me, then you are a daughter. When you feel the pain of my passion, then you are a mother having compassion on her child. When you weep for other people's troubles you are a sister and when you long to be with me in heaven, then you are a wife who has no happiness apart from her husband.'

'If you trust me you will receive my grace in abundance.'

4

Love is two-way

'I thank you for being willing to die for my love; as often as you think this, you will receive the same reward in heaven as if you had died for me. Yet you shall not be burnt by fire, drowned in water, nor harmed by the wind; nor will you be killed by any person, for your name is written on my hands and feet.'

'I am glad to have suffered pain for you. I would suffer the same pain again, just for you, rather than have you leave me. I will love you for all time even if the world rejects you – do not be afraid, they do not understand you.'

'Just as you see a child dipped in the water of baptism to cleanse it from original sin, so shall I wash all your sin away with my precious blood.'

5

Meekness

William Southfield, Carmelite friar of Norwich, said:

'Prepare yourself humbly to receive the gifts of God.'

'His mercy is always ready for us unless we turn away from him. He does not stay where he is not welcome.'

'All he asks of us is a meek and contrite heart. Our Lord himself says, "My eyes are drawn to the man of humble and contrite spirit who trembles at my word" (Isaiah 66:2).'

'I do not believe that the Lord allows anyone who places their trust in him to be continuously deceived.'

6

The Holy Spirit

William Southfield said:

'Do not resist the goodness of the Holy Spirit, for God gives his gifts where he will.'

'Believe that our Lord loves you and is working his grace in you. I pray that God will increase it and use it to his everlasting praise.'

'The Holy Spirit is active in your soul. Thank him for his goodness as we thank him for sending you to support us with your prayers. We are spared from many troubles which we would suffer for our sins if it were not for people like you among us. Praised be the Lord.'

7

Stand firm

Dame Julian said to me:

'Be obedient to the Lord and follow whatever he says. The Holy Spirit will not urge you to do anything against God or to harm other people, for that would be against his nature.'

'Virtuous people are called "the temple of the Holy Spirit" (2 Corinthians 6:16) and the Holy Spirit makes a soul firm and steady.'

'The Bible says that, "a person who doubts is like the waves of the sea when the wind drives. That sort of person, wavering between going different ways, cannot expect that the Lord will give him anything" (James 1:6–7).'

8

God within

Dame Julian says:

'Anyone who receives gifts from God should believe that the Holy Spirit dwells in his soul.'

'When God sends a person the gift of tears St Paul says they should offer them to the Lord as prayers (Romans 8:26).'

'St Jerome says, tears torment the devil more than the pains of hell. God and the devil never live together in the same place. If God is in a person's soul, the devil has no power there.'

'I pray that God will give you perseverance. Trust in God and do not worry what people say about you; the more abuse and contempt you receive in this world the greater will be your reward in heaven (Luke 6:22–23).'

9

The way God works

A Dominican anchorite at Lynn said:

'Do not be afraid of anything, our Lord will take care of you himself. Even when all your friends have deserted you he will be there.'

'For the good of your soul God has made some people to be a scourge to you. Just as a blacksmith can file rusty iron until it shines clean and bright, so the more these people try you, the brighter you will shine before God.'

'God has chosen me to look after you; be humble and courteous and thank God at all times.'

'Even if God takes away all your tears and withdraws your conversations from you, yet still you must believe that God loves you and because of the favours he has already shown you, you can be certain that you will be with him in heaven.'

10

Communion

I saw the priest hold the host above his head and the host flickered to and fro, like the wings of a dove. Then the priest held the sacrament aloft in the chalice and it moved back and forth so that it nearly fell from his hands.

Lord, as you love me, take away my sins and give me grace to receive your precious body with reverence and worship.

Within my soul I heard Jesus say, 'I know the thoughts and desires you have when you welcome me and the love you have for me when you receive my precious body. I know that sometimes your soul feels so large that you invite the whole court of heaven to come in and welcome me with flowers and sweet spices for my delight.'

11

Choosing love

Jesus spoke within my heart and said:

'No one can choose whom I love, nor how much I love them. Love defeats sin.'

'There is no better way to please God than to think continually of his love.'

'How can I love you, Lord?' I asked. He answered, 'Be aware of your sins and of my love. Do not be afraid; what a person has been in the past is not important, what matters is what they will be in the future. Remember Mary Magdalene, St Paul and many other saints, before they knew me. The dishonest I make honest, the bad I make good.'

'When I love you, I love you for ever.'

12

Forgiveness

Lord, I am sorry I have not loved you all my life. I have run away from you and you have run after me. Even when I become depressed you do not leave me.

I felt Jesus say, 'How many times have I told you that your sins are forgiven and that we will be together for ever?'

'You are a very special person to me and you will have particular grace in heaven. The whole company of heaven will be ready to welcome you.'

13

At the point of death

'You do not need to be afraid of dying in pain for I will be with you and your mind will be fixed on me.'

'I promise that you will have no more distress for I have tested you for many years with doubts and fears in your thoughts and dreams.'

'I will take your soul into my own hands which were nailed to the cross and offer it to my Father with incense and music, and you will see him.'

'I shall take you by the hand and we will dance for joy in heaven with all the saints and angels who will rejoice at your coming.'

14

The gift of tears

Lord, if you are not displeased with me, grant me a well of tears, so that I may receive the sacrament with tears of love and worship.

St Jerome appeared to me in a vision when I stood beside his tomb and said, 'Blessed are you when you weep for the sins of others, for many people will be saved by your tears. Do not be afraid, your tears are a special gift which God has given you and no person can take away.'

'There is no better way of pleasing God than to believe that he loves you. If it were possible I would weep with you for the love that I have for you and all your weeping and sorrow will turn to joy and happiness.'

15

Presence of God

I kept silence in my soul, close in the love of God.

In my soul, I felt God the Father take me by the hand and I became one with him and God the Son and the Holy Spirit.

The blessed Virgin Mary, the apostles and saints and all the angels rejoiced and prayed together.

Everywhere I heard melodious sounds, harmonies so pure that I could scarcely listen and around me I felt the presence of angels, warming me like sunbeams by day and night. I heard a voice within me say, 'Believe that it is God that speaks to you, for where God is, heaven is. God is in you and you are in God. My angels surround you so that no harm can reach you.'

16

Trust in God

The Spirit of God spoke to me and said:

'Go in the name of Jesus. I will go with you to help and support you in all you do. Trust me, you have never found me wanting. I will never ask you to do anything that is unacceptable to God.'

'I am your God and I delight in you, we shall never be parted. All the promises I have made to you will come true at the right time.'

The Lord Jesus Christ who is always ready to help and never deserts those who truly love him said, 'Do not be afraid, I will give you all you need.'

I know the Lord will help because he has never failed me wherever I have been. I have complete trust in him.

17

The Trinity

I heard the Lord say in my soul:

'Where the Holy Spirit dwells, there also is the Father and the Son; be aware of the Holy Trinity within you to give and receive love. There is still so much that you have not yet seen or felt.'

'I have chosen you to kneel before the Trinity to pray for all the world; many hundred thousand souls shall be saved by your prayers, so ask what you wish and I will give it you.'

'I know that in your soul it is as though you have prepared three cushions, one of gold, another of red velvet and the third of white silk. In your heart you think my Father sits on the gold cushion for he is all strength and power. I, Jesus, sit on the red cushion in remembrance of the blood I shed for you, and you think the Holy Spirit sits on the white cushion for he is all love and purity and the giver of all good thoughts.'

18

God cares for us

Lord Jesus Christ, in whom I place all my trust, help me and those with me to reach our homes in safety.

When I was caught in a thunderstorm Jesus said to me, 'Why are you afraid when I am with you? It is as easy for me to look after you in a field as in a cathedral.'

If God is with us we are as safe in a rowing boat as in a big ship.

When we reached land I praised God with great joy and thanked him for caring for us on the journey.

19

Provision

I felt Jesus say to me:

'Do not worry about money, you shall have all you need. Keep your mind on me and learn how to love me. I will go with you wherever you go, as I promised.'

'You are not as poor as I was when I hung on the cross for your sake. You have clothes to wear and I had none. If you urge other people to be poor for my sake you should follow your own advice.'

'Do not be afraid, I have promised that I will never fail you, my friends will look after you.'

I gave away all the money I had and some that I had borrowed, confident that God would enable me to repay it – and he did.

20

Help in trouble

The Lord said to my soul:

'There will be much trouble ahead for you, but if you wish, I can remove it.' So I prayed, Lord give me strength to bear all that it is your wish I should suffer.

'I promise that I will never leave you; the more hostility and rejection you suffer for my sake, the more I will love you. I am like a man who loves his wife; the more people abuse her, the more gifts he will lavish on her, to spite her enemies, and so I shall be with you.'

I received troubles gladly when God sent them, being pleased to feel pain for his sake. In time I became happier on the days when I suffered than on the days when there was no hardship.

21

Passion

When I see a crucifix or a person who is hurt, a child being beaten or an animal kicked, it feels in my heart like the scourging of our Lord.

On the road to Calvary I fell down and wept for it was as though I saw the crucifixion take place before my eyes. I could see Jesus hanging on the cross, his torn body covered with more wounds than a dovecote has holes. The crown of thorns pressed on his head. Rivers of blood flowed from his hands and feet nailed to the hard tree. Blood and water gushed from the hideous wound in his side – for me.

When a person dies, no one thinks it strange if their friends weep and grieve at their loss. How much more upset they might be if their friend had been wrongfully arrested and condemned to death. Would they not cry out in protest? Why then do people think it so strange that I weep for the death of our Lord?

22

A cautionary tale

There was once a priest who was lost in a wood when night fell. He found a clearing in which to rest; in the middle there was a beautiful pear tree covered with blossom. A great bear came and shook the tree so that all the flowers fell to the ground. The bear ate all the flowers then turned his back to the priest and evacuated all the flowers from his rear end. The priest, disgusted at the sight, wondered what it could mean.

The next day, walking deep in thought, he met an elderly pilgrim who asked the reason for his gloomy face. The priest told him all that had happened the previous evening, saying how much the bear's behaviour had upset him but that he did not understand the meaning.

23

Continuation

The pilgrim, who had been sent by God, gave this explanation:

You yourself are the pear tree growing and bearing flowers by saying the services and administering the sacraments. But you gabble through lauds and vespers and take Mass without proper preparation. The rest of your time is spent in making money for yourself and indulging in worldly pleasures. You break God's commandments by lying, swearing and many other sins. In other words you behave like the bear, destroying the flowers which are the good parts of your life. Unless you change your ways you will finish up in the same way as the flowers came from the bear.

24

Fruits of the spirit

Create and multiply, means to increase the fruits of the spirit which are love, joy, peace, patience, kindness, goodness, trustfulness, gentleness and self-control (Galatians 5:22).

Praised be the Lord for giving me the grace to bear malicious gossip patiently.

In my heart I heard Jesus say:

'My grace is my special gift which I give to my chosen souls whom I know will live with me for ever.'

'While your thoughts are on me you cannot sin.'

25

God in the elements

'You see how the planets follow the pattern I set and how sometimes there are thunderstorms and lightning which burns churches and houses and makes people afraid. Sometimes I send high winds which blow down steeples and uproot trees and do great damage. The wind cannot be seen but it can be felt. So it is with the Holy Spirit; it cannot be seen but it can be felt when I choose to come into a soul.'

'I come into your heart like a shaft of lightning from the sky to illuminate your soul with understanding and grace and to set you on fire with love for me.'

'You can be as sure of the love of God as you are of the sun when you see it shining brightly.'

26

Joy

Lord, you are my joy and happiness, the only treasure I have in this world. I do not wish for material goods but think only of you. My dear Lord and my God, do not leave me.

'Rejoice and be happy! If you knew how much pleasure I get from speaking to you, you would never do anything else.'

'If you said the Lord's Prayer a thousand times a day, it would not make me as glad as when you remain silent and let me speak to you.'

'You can be as sure of the love of God, as God is God. Your soul is more secure in the love of God than in your own body. Your soul will leave your body but God will never leave your soul.'

27

God in others

The Lord spoke to my heart and said:

'All the kindnesses you have done for me in your mind will receive the same reward in heaven as if you had done them in fact.'

'When you provide food or care for yourself, your family or anyone you receive in my name, it will be as though you have given it to me or my mother.'

I began to love those things which I had hated before. Now when I saw lepers through the eyes of our Lord I wanted to embrace them for the love of Jesus.

Merciful Lord Jesus Christ, you who are all love and forgiveness, look kindly on all people. Help them to know you and to be truly sorry for any wrong they have done and help them accept your forgiveness.

28

Comfort

Lord, I prayed, lift these thoughts which torment me and I will never doubt you again.

God sent an angel to comfort me who said, 'God has not forsaken you. He will never forget his promise but because you did not believe it was the Holy Spirit speaking in your soul, he has allowed you to be punished.'

I will lie still and listen to your voice.

Then I was filled with joy for I heard the Lord speak to me as he had before. Lord, I will believe that every good thought comes from you; do not leave me again.

29

Revealing love

'In this world, you cannot know how much I love you for your heart could not contain the joy, so I show you just a small part of my love.'

'In the next world you shall know how much I loved you on earth; then you will be able to see all the days I spent with you and the love I gave you for other people. This will be your reward in heaven.'

'You know that the devil has no kindness. He is angry with you and might hurt you a little but he shall not harm you, except perhaps in making you a little afraid, so that you pray even more to me for grace and direct all your life to me.'

30

Worship

I wept with joy when I saw the holy sacrament carried through the town with all the people kneeling in reverence.

If I saw a prince or a bishop or important person whom people bowed to and revered I could only think of our Lord and the joy with which all the angels bowed down to worship him.

I pray that I may be joined to our Lord through my love for him, that I may be given the grace to love, worship and praise him. To love only what he loves and to want only what he wants and always be ready to do as he wishes by day or night gladly, without complaining.

31

Doubt

I felt that God had forsaken me or I would not have been tempted.

We receive a wealth of grace except when we doubt or distrust God, allowing bitter and unkind thoughts into our hearts. Only the mercy of God restores us to his grace.

Sometimes I was in great sadness for I did not know if my feelings were from God or if they were deceits or illusions. I had no peace until I knew if they were true.

Blessed be God who gave me strength to persevere.

I prayed for understanding.

32

Suffering for God

If I saw an animal being punished I would think it should have been me that was being punished for my unkindness to God.

I endured all the abuse patiently because I knew that people had been far more unkind to Jesus when he had been here on earth.

Jesus said, 'I know how much you suffer from the insults and cruel words which are said to you. Do not worry about anything that people say. Because you have suffered so much for me you will have great joy in heaven.'

'I thank you because it distresses you when anyone breaks my commandments or swears by my name and because you are always ready to rebuke them for love of me.'

33

God with us

My mind and my heart gradually became so joined to God that he was continually with me in everything that lived. The more my love grew, the more I became aware of my own sins and my dependence upon God.

Lying in my bed I heard the Lord call my name. I listened in silence until he spoke.

'Where God is, heaven is. God is in your soul night and day.'

'When you go to church I go with you; when you sit down for a meal I sit with you; when you lie down to sleep I lie with you and when you go out I go with you.'

34

Getting to know you

'I thank you for allowing me to work my will in you and that you will let me talk to you so easily. Nothing that you do on earth can please me so much as letting me speak to your soul; in that way I get to know you and you learn to know me.'

I was sad because I could not understand the sermons that were preached, then within my soul I heard Jesus say, 'I will talk with you and teach you myself for your thoughts and meditations are agreeable to me.'

'For every time you receive the sacrament with your thoughts centred on me, you will receive more joy in heaven.'

35

Rest in God

In my soul I heard Jesus say, 'If you will love me with all your heart then I may rest there. If you allow me to rest in your heart on earth then believe me when I tell you that you will rest with me in heaven.'

'I ask no more of you than that you love me as I love you.'

'You know that when you have received me into your soul you are in peace and quiet.'

'I would speak to you more often than you will let me.'

'I would take you by the hand so that people know that you are my friend.'

36

Love for others

I love God above all things and I love God in all people.

Every day my love of the Lord increased. The more my love grew, the greater was my sorrow for the sins of the people.

In my heart I heard Jesus say, 'I thank you for loving all the people who are in the world today and all those who are to come. I thank you for your concern that they should all be saved and your willingness to suffer or to die if it would help them and please me.'

37

Tears of love

Jesus said, 'You know that at times I send heavy rain and sharp showers and at other times gentle drops, so it is when I speak to your soul. Sometimes I give you gentle weeping and soft tears as a token that I love you, and at other times I give you loud cries and shrieks to make people afraid for the grace I have given you.'

'I want you to know that because of the pain you feel when you weep for love of me, you will feel no pain when you leave this world. As you have had compassion for my body, so I must have compassion for your body.'

Lord Jesus, it feels so good to weep for you on earth, I know that it will be joyful to be with you in heaven. Lord, let me have no other joy on earth than weeping for your love. If I were in hell I would weep for you there as I do now, and so hell would become a kind of heaven for your love overcomes all fear. I would rather be there if it would please you than in this world and displease you. Lord, as you wish, so may it be.

38

Our Lady

Mary, the Mother of God, rested in my soul and said, 'I bring you greetings from my son Jesus and all the angels and saints in heaven. I will be a mother to you, to teach you how to please God.'

'Do not be afraid to accept the gifts my son will give you.'

'If you would share in our love you must also share in our sorrow.'

Glorious Queen of heaven, anyone who has you for a friend will be greatly blessed, for when you pray, the whole company of heaven prays with you.

39

Reassurance

Jesus said, 'When your spiritual father tells you that you have displeased God, you should believe him and repent until you receive grace again.'

'I cannot bear to leave you in pain for any length of time so I come to reassure you of my love.'

'There is nothing so certain on this earth as my love for you. Do not forget me for I never forget you and I keep constant watch over you.'

'You have good reason to love me well, there is nothing I want so much as the love of your heart.'

'If you will do as I ask, I will do as you ask.'

40

In touch with God

Jesus said, 'Nobody on earth can know how you commune with me, even you can hardly understand your feelings for me. It is foolish for people in the world to judge you when only God knows what is in your heart.'

'Sometimes I am hidden in your soul. I withdraw until you feel that you have no goodness in yourself and you know that all goodness comes from me. Then you know what pain it is to be without me and the joy it is to feel me with you and it makes you eager to seek me again.'

'You have good reason to rejoice and be happy in your soul; my love for you is so great that I cannot withdraw it.'

'Every good thought you have in your heart is the word of God, even if at times you do not hear me clearly.'

Purification

On the day of purification, which is Candlemas, all the people were in church with their candles and in contemplation I saw our Lady with Joseph offering her son to Simeon, the priest in the temple. I heard songs so beautiful that I was transported with love for our Lord and could not hold my candle to offer to the priest.

Every time I see women being purified after childbirth it is as though I see our Lady.

When I watch a wedding, in my heart I see our Lady joined with St Joseph and the joining of a soul with Jesus Christ our Lord.

When I see children carried in their mothers' arms it seems to me I see Christ in his childhood.

42

Prayer

In meditation I heard the Lord say, 'Which seems to you the better prayer, to pray to me with your heart or with your thoughts?'

'When you pray with your thoughts you know what you ask me and you understand what I say to you. When you sit still and give your heart to meditation, then you will receive thoughts that God has put into your mind.'

'I accept all your prayers whether you speak them, think in your heart, read, or listen to reading.'

'Fasting, penance and saying the daily offices are good when you are learning to pray, and I accept any form of prayer gladly, but you are much closer to me when you sit quietly in contemplation.'

43

Deserving love

Jesus Christ is my love.

'You say that I should be called all good and say that you will find that I am all good to you. You say I deserve to be called all love and you will find that I love you for I know every thought in your heart.'

Blessed may you be, Lord, for you do what you tell me to do. You tell me to love my enemies (Matthew 5:44) and I know that I have been your worst enemy. If I were killed a hundred times a day I could never show you the love you have shown me. Jesus said to me, 'Give me nothing but love, there is no better way to please me than to keep me always in your love. Think of me wherever you are and whatever you do, for I know every thought that passes through your mind and every twinkle in your eye.'

44

A journey

I asked the Lord if I should go on a journey; he said, 'Go in my name. I will go with you and bring you back in safety.'

The Lord sent storms so fierce that we expected to be shipwrecked and commended ourselves and our ship to the care of the Lord.

Lord, I came on this journey for love of you and you have promised that I shall be safe. Remember your promises and show me that it was you who directed me to come and not some evil spirit who has led me astray.

The Lord answered me, 'Why are you afraid? Why do you not trust me? I am as powerful on the sea as on the land.'

'I will keep my promises to you. Wait patiently and trust me. Do not waver in your faith for without faith you grieve me. If you trust and do not doubt you will gain peace of mind and strength to comfort those with you who are in fear and sorrow.'

45

Dreams

In a dream I saw the body of our Lord lying in front of me. His head was close beside me, his face towards me. Then I saw someone come with a dagger and cut that precious body right across the breast.

In another dream I saw the Lord standing close beside me so near that I put my hand on his toes and felt the flesh and bone.

And again I saw our Lady with a white scarf in her hand, saying, 'Will you see my son?' Then I saw our Lady take her son in her arms and wrap him in the white scarf.

The book of life

One time, when I prayed before the cross on the altar I fell asleep and in a dream I saw an angel, a child dressed in white, carrying a large book. I said to the child, 'This is the book of life.' I looked in the book and saw the Trinity all in gold. Then I said, 'Where is my name?' The child answered, 'Your name is written at the foot of the Trinity,' and then he was gone.

Our Lord Jesus Christ spoke to me and said, 'Be sure that you are loyal and constant and that your faith is strong, for your name is written in heaven in the book of life. The angel came to give you comfort. You should be happy and keep your heart on me and increase your love of God. If you follow God's advice you will do nothing wrong, for God's advice is to be meek and patient in love.'

47

Appearances

Do not judge a person by their outward appearance. Only God knows what is in their soul.

Jesus said, 'I thank you because you wish that all people should love me and that they would give as much time and thought to loving me as they do to earning a living.'

'I know that you have wished for great wealth so that you could give it away, in my name. I accept your thoughts as the gifts you would have given.'

In my heart I said, 'I wish I were as deserving of your love as Mary Magdalene.' Our Lord answered, 'I love you just as well and I give you the same peace as I gave her. No saint in heaven minds when I love a person on earth as much as I love them.'

48

Obedience

Follow where the Spirit leads you in the name of Jesus.

I had no rest or peace in my soul until I agreed to do as the Spirit moved me.

My son said, 'Through your prayers I have come to know the Lord and by the grace of God I shall follow your advice more than I have done before.'

I thanked God many times for answering my prayers.

49

Hearing the Spirit

Every time I hear a robin sing, I am filled with thankfulness and praise.

One day in church I was surrounded by such a sweet atmosphere I felt that if it continued I could live without food and drink.

I heard a noise like wind blowing in my ears and knew it for the sound of the Holy Spirit which became like the voice of a dove.

When the Lord spoke to me I lost all sense of time. I did not know if he was with me five or six hours or only one. It was so holy and full of grace that I felt as if I had been in heaven.

50

Decisions

I went into church and prayed earnestly for guid-ance in the answer I should give.

Lord, you know all things; you know I do not want to do wrong. Show me what I should do.

I gave praise and thanks to God for his mercy and goodness, more particularly because he had told me that all would be well when it seemed that only a miracle could make it right.

The people knew that God had answered my prayers.

Holy Thursday

As I walked in procession, it seemed to me that our Lady, St Mary Magdalene and the twelve apostles walked with me. I saw how our Lady said farewell to her son. He kissed her and all the apostles and Mary Magdalene. It was a parting full of both sorrow and joy.

Good Friday

The priest lifted the veil three times so that the people could venerate the crucifix. I felt my soul lifted above all earthly things to worship him who is both God and man.

Ascension Day

It seemed that I saw the Lord ascend into heaven. I wished so much that I could go with him for I did not know what I would do without him here on earth. All my happiness and joy was with him and I knew that I would not be content until I was with him.

52

Jesus comforts his Mother

In my soul, I saw our Lord Jesus Christ kneel for his mother's blessing and I heard her say, 'My son, I have no happiness in this world except you. If you will, let me die before you so that I may not endure the sorrow of your death. If you have no thought for yourself, have thought for your mother for you know no one can comfort me except you.' Our Lord took his mother in his arms and said, 'Do not mourn. I have told you many times that unless I die, no one can be saved. It is my Father's will, let it also be yours. My death will become great joy to you and to all people. You must remain after me for the holy Church will be built on your faith. By your faith the Church will increase her faith. I have promised that you will be with me in heaven and there you shall be queen and all the angels and saints will be obedient to you. I have told you that when the time comes for you to join me, I will come to fetch you myself with my angels and saints and we will bring you before my Father with great rejoicing.'

53

Jesus comforts Margery

When I saw all this in my soul, I fell at the feet of Jesus asking him to bless me and in my mind I cried, 'Lord, what shall I do? I would rather that you killed me than let me stay in this world without you.' He answered, 'Stay with my mother and comfort her. Find your comfort in her for she cannot escape this sorrow. I will come again and turn your sorrow into joy.' Then it seemed our Lord left us. I went to our Lady and said, 'Come, blessed Lady, let us follow your son for as long as we can until he dies. Dear Lady, how can you bear to see your son bear this ordeal? My heart is breaking yet I am not his mother.' Our Lady turned to me and said, 'You heard how there can be no other way. I cannot avoid suffering for love of my son.'

54

The betrayal

In my heart, we followed our Lord and watched while he prayed on the Mount of Olives. We saw how our Lord woke his disciples. A great crowd of people approached carrying lights and armed with swords and sticks. Jesus said to them, 'Who are you looking for?' and they answered, 'Jesus of Nazareth.' Our Lord said, 'I am he.'

Judas kissed our Lord and the soldiers seized him roughly. In great wretchedness we watched as Jesus was dragged away. We wept to see the cruel way they treated our Lord; they spat in his face, pulled his ears and his beard. They dragged off his clothes as if he had been a common criminal and he said not a word.

In my soul I heard our Lord say, 'I have suffered these pains for love of you. More pain than any man on earth. You have good cause to love me for I have bought your love dearly.'

55

The scourging

In contemplation, I saw our Lord tied to a pillar, his hands fastened above his head. I saw sixteen men, each with a scourge; every scourge had eight pellets of lead on the end and each pellet was covered in spikes like the rowel of a spur. The men agreed between themselves that they should each give our Lord forty strokes. I wept out loud at this terrible sight.

When our Lord had been beaten they released him and gave him his cross to carry on his shoulder. It seemed that I went a different way with our Lady and when we saw Jesus again he was in great pain from the weight of the cross. Our Lady said, 'My son, let me help you,' but she fell to the ground from weakness and our Lord knelt to comfort his mother.

56

The crucifixion

Again in contemplation, I saw the place where our Lord Jesus Christ was nailed to the cross. I saw them tear a silk cloth from our Lord's body which had stuck with congealed blood. The skin tore away, leaving his body raw and running with blood. The cruel men took a long nail and drove it through one hand with violent blows and his precious body contracted with pain. Then in my soul, I saw how they fastened ropes to the other hand and pulled it into place, for the sinews had so shrunk that it would not reach the hole they had made ready. And then they dragged his feet down in the same way.

I heard our Lady cry out, 'My son never did you any harm, why do you treat him so?' And I thought I cried, 'Why do you kill my Lord Jesus Christ? Kill me instead and let him go.'

57

Jesus dies

In my mind I saw our Lord hanging on the cross and I heard him say to his mother, 'Here is your son.' St John took our Lady into his arms to comfort her. It seemed I said, 'Lord, what shall we do now? How shall we bear this great grief we have for love of you?'

Our Lord said to one thief, 'This day shalt thou be with me in paradise.' I prayed to our Lord that he would be as merciful to my soul when I came to leave this world as he had been to the thief, for I thought I was worse than any thief.

Our Lord commended his soul into his Father's hands and then he died.

I thought our Lady fell fainting to the ground. I thought I ran around like a mad woman, roaring and crying. I knelt by our Lady and said to her, 'Do not be so distressed, your son has no more pain now. Let me grieve for you, for your sorrow is my sorrow.'

58

Jesus is taken down from the cross

In contemplation, I saw Joseph of Arimathea take our Lord's body from the cross and lay it on a marble stone in front of our Lady. Our Lady knelt by the body of her son and washed the blood from his face with her tears.

Mary Magdalene wept by our Lord's feet and the sisters of our Lady each took a hand to hold and kiss. I felt in my heart that I would lose my reason, I so longed to be alone with the body of our Lord to weep and mourn.

I saw Joseph of Arimathea and St John the Evangelist come to bury the body of our Lord but our Lady said, 'Would you take my son from me? If you must bury his body, bury me with him for I do not know how to live without him.' I thought I spoke to our Lady so gently that she consented to let them bury her son as it was right for them to do.

59

St Peter's sorrow

In contemplation, I saw our Lady go homeward.
I heard her cry out, 'Where is my son?' and heard
St John answer, 'Lady, you know that he is dead.'

I heard St Peter knocking at the door but he would
not come in. I saw St Peter kneel in tears before
our Lady and I heard him say, 'Lady, I beg your
forgiveness. I denied my master, your son who
loved me. I do not deserve to look on him or you
again.'

Our Lady answered, 'Do not be afraid, Peter; even
if you forsook him, he has not abandoned you.
He has promised that he will come again on the
third day to comfort me.'

60

The Lord is risen

In contemplation, I stayed with our Lady and it seemed a thousand years until the third day. When that day came, our Lord Jesus Christ appeared and greeted his mother. I heard our Lord say, 'I have no more pain and I shall live for evermore. Your pain and sorrow will become joy and happiness.'

Afterwards, in my heart, I saw Mary Magdalene grieving by the tomb. I saw how our Lord appeared to her like a gardener and said, 'Woman, why weepest thou?' Mary, not recognizing him, said, 'If you have taken away my Lord, tell me where I can find him?' Jesus took pity on her and said, 'Mary'. With that one word she knew him.

Every time I heard the story of the Passion I wept as if I would have died for love of our Lord, so much did I long to be with him.

61

The mirror of love

Jesus said to Margery:

'I have chosen you to be a mirror to the people that they may follow your example and show sorrow for their sins so that they may be saved.'

62

Margery's prayer

For all graces which are needful to me and to all the creatures on earth, and for all those that have faith and trust, or shall have faith and trust, in my prayers until the world's end, such grace as they desire, ghostly or bodily, to the profit of their souls, I pray thee, Lord, grant them, for the multitude of thy mercy. Amen.

Suggestions for further reading

The Book of Margery Kempe, edited by W. Butler-Bowdon. Oxford University Press 1954

Margery Kempe; Genius and Mystic, Catherine Cholmeley. Longmans 1947

Mystic and Pilgrim; The Book and World of Margery Kempe, C. W. Atkinson. Cornell University Press 1983

Women in Medieval Life, Margaret Wade Labage. Hamish Hamilton 1986

The Medieval Mystical Tradition in England, ed. Marion Glasscoe. D. S. Brewer 1984

Margery Kempe; An Example in the English Pastoral Tradition, Martin Thornton. SPCK 1960

The Book of Margery Kempe, trans. B. A. Windeatt. Penguin 1985

Sources and index

The extracts have been taken from *The Book of Margery Kempe*, edited by W. Butler-Bowdon (1954), by permission of Oxford University Press. To assist the devotional aspect, the passages in this book have been presented in the first person instead of using Margery's reference to herself as "that creature". The English has been modernized throughout with the exception of the prayer on p. 76.

The index which follows shows the chapter from which each Reading is taken. Each numbered reading in this book is in bold type and is followed by the chapter numbers in *The Book*, in the order in which the Readings appear on the page.